Dear Ceinwen,

Thank you so much interest in my work, ...
it.

Best wishes, Helen.

Light is a prayer

CW00550799

Light is a prayer

by

Helen Openshaw

First published 2024 by The Hedgehog Poetry Press,

5 Coppack House, Churchill Avenue, Clevedon. BS21 6QW

www.hedgehogpress.co.uk

ISBN: 978-1-916830-23-3

Cover image: Hubble Goes High Def to Revisit the Iconic 'Pillars of
Creation' Messier 16 (The Eagle Nebula). Original from NASA. Digitally
enhanced by rawpixel.

To Petra - my dearest, lifelong friend - in memory of our Florence adventure.

Contents

Spring Wedding 9

Our Journey Ahead 10

Night Jazz 11

The Heartbeat of the city 12

My Very Excellent Friend 13

First Signs of Summer 14

Wensleydale Road 15

The Longest Month 16

Finding Treasure 17

Can you see the light? 18

Under the Shelter of a dandelion sun, ... 19

Watching the sunset from an aeroplane window 20

SPRING WEDDING

We are all brides in waiting,
Spring, our wedding.

Through Winter,
falling leaves become trinkets
in a box I keep for secrets.

I make the trees my jewels.
Growth buds, delicate
earrings for the day.
The crown, a tiara,
weeping the loss of innocence.
The snowdrops at the base,
                    my bouquet.

OUR JOURNEY AHEAD

Soon we will visit the bones of the city,
feast on the very heart and soul,
until it sings in our veins.
We do not know yet of its power,
how the place will hold our view,
a magnet pulling at every sense -
It's touch no heavier than breath.

NIGHT JAZZ

Voices trail on the night air.
A lullaby song drifts,
a piano plays out the last
notes of the day,
and a saxophone rift dances
us into the night,
on dreams that carry our voices
across the star strewn sky.

THE HEARTBEAT OF THE CITY

Bells frame the city,
paint the stories of visitors,
the ancient stones worn smooth
by their steps.
In communion with the rhythm,
my spinning top mind,
folds,
tumbles,
turns and twists
across the fire topped roofs.

MY VERY EXCELLENT FRIEND

I had forgotten your laugh,
the whoop light joy of it,
how we breakfast on memories
to fuel the day together.

We find a holiday catchphrase,
sing and embarrass the kids,
an earworm that returns to me
weeks later
and makes me miss you more.

We lit candles for loved ones,
remembered their light and shade.
The shape of who we are,
mirrored in smiles and glances,
the flame still reflected in our eyes.

FIRST SIGNS OF SUMMER

The liquid trill of the blackbird,
a river surfing our senses,
I dip and drown on the warm
 butter scent of summer.

A sea of blue – the bells are ringing
in the season, on a tumbling wave
of Cow Parsley.
Time laced and locked.

WENSLEYDALE ROAD

Grandma is in her kitchen,
the blue hope of the day
pressing at the window.
The smell of coffee,
sharp and full.

Her bustling spirit
attacking the chores,
twin tub blues
the only dampener on our
perfect time together.

Tea bread rising in the oven,
calms the anxious moments,
ironing out worries and stress.
As we dive out of the door,
equipped with tartan
flasks and rugs,
for tea picnics and feeding the ducks -

There is Grandad - quiet and still -
my hand secure in his.

THE LONGEST MONTH

Darkness hasn't finished with us yet.
It folds, and folds again,
squeezing us into corners,
pressing every sense, tomb'd
in days that suffocate.

I long to breathe the sunrise,
but a blindfold is tied by my captive,
as I sit out winter's sentence,
waiting for Persephone's roots
to birth me into the light.

FINDING TREASURE

Birthing the day,
I treasure seek in a pale light,
and dive into the topaz blue.

The sky a cracked shell
gifts in my hand a pearl moon,
Aphrodite's tear.

Now my mind is
uncaged, untethered.
I swim in joy and smile at
the secret I keep.

CAN YOU SEE THE LIGHT?

The night has a snag,
a rip and a seam,
cut through by the wind;
moon- tethered and carved.

Are we just orphans in the storm,
taken hostage in a sky
drawn to blindness?

I tell you,
even shadows hold some light.

UNDER THE SHELTER OF A DANDELION SUN,

I saw you hold it
like a searchlight for home.
The seeds blown wayward,
summer a wish, a hum.

Memories hidden in a seashell,
burrowed and safe,
this golden glow, we didn't know
we were part of, until it had gone.

Our souls upturned as the forest
enveloped us,
fears shrunk by each
story you tell, as many as the
seeds that float like stars
on the rising dawn.
We dwell again.

WATCHING THE SUNSET FROM AN AEROPLANE WINDOW

We chase the light and lines
of setting suns,
each one full, our eyes
fresh to its understanding of
untold stories we long to hear.

The spiced orange fullness
shakes the blue,
ripples the approaching night
until it falls under the spell
you weave – lacing the sky
with studded stars
that hold our gaze.

Sand dunes of ginger, nutmeg,
a dragon's tongue of fire
feasting on the innocence
              of the moment.

Watching, thirsting
for the last symphony of the day,
       the last sinking rays,
a dying volcano,
       a flickering candle flame.